A DAY THAT MADE HISTORY

SHARPEVILLE

Sarah Harris

Dryad Press Limited   London

Contents

THE EVENTS

THE INVESTIGATION

Acknowledgements

Special thanks go to Charles Freeman whose unpublished Sixth Form World Studies Project on the Shooting at Sharpeville gave the idea and much information for this book.

The author and publishers thank the following for their kind permission to reproduce copyright illustrations: International Defence and Aid Fund, pages 4, 5, 6, 8, 9, 10, 13, 14, 17, 18, 20, 24, 29, 35, 36, 39, 46, 49, 52, 55, 57, 59, 60; The Keystone Collection, pages 26, 32, 37, 48, 53; Sunday Times, page 21. The maps on pages 30, 31 and 35 are by R. F. Brien. The pictures were researched by David Pratt.

The "Day that Made History" series was devised by Nathaniel Harris.

Typeset by Latimer Trend & Co Ltd, Plymouth, and printed and bound by Anchor Brendon Ltd, Tiptree for the publishers, Dryad Press Limited, 8 Cavendish Square, London W1M 0AJ

ISBN 0 8521 9767 5

THE
EVENTS

At the police station: 1.00–1.40 p.m., 21st March, 1960

The police station consisted of several buildings and a big yard, all surrounded by a wire fence. To the north was a large field; to the west, a square; and to the south, across the street, began neat rows of small houses. By about 1 o'clock there were many policemen about. Roughly 200 police were inside the wire fence and there were a few more outside. Gathered all around the police station was a crowd of the town's residents, perhaps somewhere in the region of 10,000 people. The figure was probably much less; it could have been more.

In charge of the police was Lieutenant Colonel Pienaar. He was in a bad temper. One of the crowd outside the station had thrown a stone which had hit his car as he had arrived with some reinforcements at about 1 o'clock. As far as he was concerned, the crowd outside was a mob, ready for anything. Before coming to the police station, he had had a word with Major Van Zyl, who had been in command there in the morning. Major Van Zyl had told him that he would be arriving to face a dangerous situation. Lt. Col. Pienaar was under the impression that the crowd had been troublesome and violent all morning and had failed to disperse when charged with batons and tear gas. He was not prepared to stand much more of this nonsense.

Most of the police were armed. They had Sten guns, revolvers and rifles, and they sat on their Saracen armoured cars, of which there were about six in the compound, or stood around in small groups waiting for instructions. The crowd was growing as more and more of the townspeople arrived to

Police vehicles approach the police station at Sharpeville on the morning of 21st March, 1960. A crowd has already begun to gather outside the gate.

see what was happening. Becoming impatient, people began to press against the fence and the noise grew louder and louder. Among the crowd great shouts of "Our land!" could be heard. It is possible that some of the police began to feel uncomfortable, tense, even frightened. They were not used to facing confident, good-tempered crowds, as this one generally was.

At about 1.30 Lt. Col. Pienaar decided to position about 70 of his policemen along the perimeter fence of the station. They had with them their machine guns and rifles, which many of them had already fully loaded, and they formed a straggly line along the west and south sides of the compound, inside the fence; no-one seems to have been put in charge. The Saracen cars were stationed on the north side, with their crews sitting or standing on the roofs. Shortly afterwards, Lt. Col. Pienaar told the policemen to load five rounds of ammunition. He knew many of them had already loaded their guns, but he thought the order might frighten the crowd and that his men would realize that they were only to shoot that number of rounds if or when the order to fire was given.

Meanwhile the Special Branch Officer, Colonel Spengler, had begun arresting one or two of the organizers of the

The Saracen armoured cars are now inside the compound of the police station, their guns trained on the crowd outside, which is pressing hard against the fence.

demonstration. When he ordered the gates to be opened, so as to bring in the people he wished to detain, there was no difficulty in shutting them again. The crowd did not seem to want to enter the compound.

Joshua Motha, who was in the crowd standing near the main entrance, was under the impression that everyone was feeling rather pleased. From what people were saying, the police were going to make an announcement that would sort out the disagreements, and then everyone could go home. When a big grey police car and three Saracen armoured cars drew up to the gate and were let into the police station, Joshua Motha and his friends thought that the official who was to make the announcement must have arrived. One of the cars may have slightly injured one of the crowd, but no-one seems to have taken any notice of it. Everyone was busy moving in to hear the long-awaited statement. As the police lined up by the fence with their guns, those in front of the crowd assumed that they were forming a kind of guard of honour for the important official.

Not very far away, Lechael Musibi cycled towards the deserted school where he was a teacher, to collect some books he had left there. None of the students had turned up to lessons that day, and so the school had been closed. Realizing that he had left his keys with a student in another part of town, he changed direction and set off to fetch them. His route took him along the road outside the police station.

The crowd was growing larger and larger. A few children started to throw stones and shout slogans. Two or three more people at the front were arrested, but when the gates were opened to admit the policeman and those arrested there was still no attempt to break in to the compound: the townspeople continued to shout and roar and press forward, apparently without any definite intention, waiting for the "meeting" to begin. To Lt. Col. Pienaar, they seemed to be in a state of frenzy.

Suddenly, somewhere close to the police station, some people heard a sudden loud noise. A newspaper photographer nearby thought it was a shot, but no-one knew what the sound really was. Others just heard the voice of a policeman saying "Fire!" Others heard neither. For whatever reason, the police began to fire their machine guns, revolvers and rifles. Within a matter of seconds, 69 people in the crowd were dead or dying and another 180 wounded: the time was 1.40 p.m., the day Monday, 21st March, 1960, the place Sharpeville in South Africa.

The debris of death. The scene outside the police station a few minutes after the shooting stopped.

Sharpeville that morning

The people of Sharpeville

With a population of about 36,000, Sharpeville was a large, sprawling township built for black South Africans who worked in the neighbouring white area of Vereeniging, an Afrikaner town in the Transvaal. All black South Africans had to live in areas of the country approved for them by the white government. This meant either one of the "homelands", areas set aside many years before where blacks could own land, or one of the large urban developments outside white towns. The homelands were now badly overcrowded, over-exploited and poverty-stricken, and in the townships housing standards were abysmally low and facilities almost non-existent. But at least in these townships there was the possibility of paid employment in the nearby areas where whites lived or in the industries of the white economy. The right of blacks to live and work in white areas was regulated by the pass, a document which all black South Africans had to carry at all times.

For many years Sharpeville had been regarded as a "model" township. Living conditions were marginally better than in some other black townships, though there was still extensive poverty. The wages of black South Africans were so low that an independent survey concluded in 1959 that the majority of African families had £10 a month less to live on than the minimum required to maintain a family adequately.

Earlier in 1960 rents in the Sharpeville township had been raised, with no compensating rise in wages. On Monday, 21st March, also, a government directive that would force skilled black building workers to become labourers was to be implemented in the Transvaal. Bricklayers, plasterers and other craftsmen could face a reduction of wages from £15.50 per week to £3.25, as the government pursued its policy of reserving all skilled jobs for whites.

All this meant that in Sharpeville there was a great deal of support for the newly-formed Pan-African Congress (P.A.C.), which promised to pursue a vigorous campaign to restore South Africa to its African people.

That morning, the local P.A.C. leaders, Tsolo and More, and several hundred of their supporters prepared to take part in the nationwide protest which had been called earlier that

This is Soweto (South West Township), one of the African townships for Johannesburg, to the north of Vereeniging. The featureless lines of identical housing, with corrugated iron roofs and little rooms, are common to African townships throughout South Africa.

month by Robert Sobukwe. The protest was to be against the pass book, the document which controlled the lives of the residents of Sharpeville and of every other black African in South Africa who moved outside the boundaries of the "homelands". In this pass book were recorded details of name, address, date of birth and place of birth, which tribal grouping the holder belonged to, and his or her place of work. Official stamps showed that the holder of this little book had the right to live in "white" South Africa, work in white areas and travel into white residential areas to carry out that work.

Each of the protesters carefully left the pass book at home and stepped out into the street. Just by doing so they committed a crime. Some of them went about Sharpeville telling their neighbours not to go to work and explaining that this was a great day of protest. Others went to the buses that would have taken the Africans to their work in Vereeniging and persuaded the drivers not to run them. Sometimes threats as well as a few friendly words were needed to make sure that everyone would join the protest, but on the whole the people of the township wanted to join and were eager to help.

Inside the houses of the townships overcrowding is a real problem. Often more than one nuclear family unit has to share a two-bedroomed, one living-roomed house.

Assured of widespread support, the protesters began walking towards the police station, where they were to offer themselves for arrest. Being found without a pass meant that you were liable to be fined, imprisoned or to have your right to live outside the "homelands" taken away from you. The protesters all knew this, but carried on nevertheless, deliberately inviting arrest. Once taken into custody, they intended to refuse bail, to refuse to pay any fines and, if released, to ask to be re-arrested. They hoped to disrupt the pass law system so much that the government would be forced to abandon it. To get rid of the pass would remove one of the greatest weapons against black South Africans and one of the most effective controls the whites held. With the pass gone, families could be reunited, people could move about freely to look for work, and there would no longer be the fear of being thrown out of your home if illness or injury prevented you from working and you therefore lost your pass. People were encouraged by memories of earlier actions, such as the great protests of women in the 1920s which had so disrupted the system that for years women were exempt from the pass laws.

As they made their way to the police station, the original

Robert Sobukwe, the leader of the Pan-African Congress, walks at the front of his supporters on the way to seek imprisonment for defying the pass laws.

protesters were joined by new recruits. Since the buses were not running, and it was impossible to go to work, even the politically uninvolved thought they might as well go along too. Women joined them. Children did not go to school. At the gates of the police station the leaders demanded arrest.

Joshua Motha had had a busy night, first of all hiding his bus so that it could not be used to drive people to work in Vereeniging and then going to the police station to tell them why he would not be going to work. As the police took no notice of his report, he went home to have some breakfast, but before he could finish it, the young P.A.C. organizers were wanting him back at the police station. Grumbling to them and to himself, he left his breakfast half eaten. He stayed at the police station on and off all morning, listening, waiting and watching.

Lechael Musibi had gone to school as usual that morning, but none of his students turned up. Having stayed around for a while, he set off for home again at about half past ten. He heard that, at about 2 o'clock, someone important would be making an announcement at the police station. As he was on his way home, a number of aeroplanes flew low over Sharpeville and dived towards the crowd that was beginning to surround the police station. The children thought this was great fun and cheered them wildly.

Rumours began flying around the township that a "big boss" from Pretoria was going to address the crowd at 2 o'clock and that the *dompas* would be abolished. More and more people flocked to the station. There was, after all, little else to do. By 1.00 p.m. several thousand people were there. Mr Labuschagne, the Location Superintendent (the white man appointed by the government to run the township), walked through the crowd towards the police station. Many people greeted him cheerfully and he stopped to chat to one or two on his way in.

The police

The authorities had known for two days that 21st March was to be the day of protest which the P.A.C. had been promising to call for some time. When it became clear that the protest was of a significant size in Sharpeville, police reinforcements were sent there from Vereeniging and Lt. Col. Pienaar, an experienced Afrikaner officer, was put in charge.

Crowd control was not something of which the South African police had much experience. People were not usually allowed to protest for long in South Africa. Normally, the police operated under orders to break up protests and demonstrations in an effective way, not to manage them. By the time Lt. Col. Pienaar arrived at the police compound the crowd was too large, and the police were too hemmed in, for the usual techniques of charging with their batons, whips and armoured cars to have much effect. Even in the morning, when the crowd was smaller, no-one seems to have thought of employing those techniques at any stage. Tear-gas canisters were usually available to the police, but although the subsequent police statement said that tear gas was employed at Sharpeville that morning but failed to disperse the crowd, all other witnesses agree that it was never used and never threatened. Indeed, it appears that the police never actually asked the crowd to disperse in any way.

When Lt. Col. Pienaar deployed his men around the compound, he was motivated by several mistaken ideas. He thought that he was coming to face a dangerous situation, and that tear gas, threats and bullets fired over the crowd had

Dillwyn Llewelyn School

failed to move them. He did not ask for further details from any of the policemen who had been there all morning, but proceeded to act like a frightened man. Perhaps Lt. Col. Pienaar and some of his men had in mind an incident that had happened a couple of months before in Durban, when black Africans, angered by persistent police raids on their beer halls, had turned on them and killed nine; five black and four white policemen. Perhaps they were unnerved at facing a protest that was dignified, purposeful and at the same time illegal, especially a protest held by blacks, whom most South African whites regarded with a mixture of hatred, contempt and fear. As they stood there, on a mild autumn day, with their loaded guns, it may have seemed to many policemen that the situation was becoming more dangerous with every moment.

Independent witnesses

There were not many independent witnesses to the scenes in Sharpeville that day. On the whole, the international newspapers were not interested in covering this event. Like many other black protests, it was of little concern to white South Africans, as they were confident that there would be no change to the system which ran their country or to the rights and privileges they enjoyed. They had great confidence in the government of their Prime Minister, Dr Verwoerd. One reporter who was present was Humphrey Tyler, a white journalist reporting for a black magazine called *The Drum*. During his drive into Sharpeville there was nothing to warn him of what was to happen soon. Children were waving, and people were grinning as Tyler drove into Sharpeville behind the police armoured cars. It all had the atmosphere of a Sunday School outing.

Accompanying Humphrey Tyler was a photographer, and several other newspaper photographers were at the scene too. Tyler's account of the sight that greeted him in Sharpeville, supported by the series of pictures taken that morning, make it hard for us to conjure up the image of a "wild" crowd, out of control and threatening the lives of Lt. Col. Pienaar's policemen.

After the shootings

Joshua Motha was not frightened when he heard the first shots being fired. He thought they were blanks. Then he saw a fellow African lying on the ground and at the same moment felt a bullet graze his trousers. As the truth dawned on him, he turned to flee and another bullet entered his hip. He fell where he was. Lechael Musibi was aware of the crowd running towards him and that he was falling from his bicycle. He thought, at first, that he had been knocked off by the crowd. As he tried to get up, the shooting started again and so he lay flat on the ground watching as people fell all around him. When silence eventually returned he picked himself up and made his way to the library, where a little girl shouted "Look! He is shot!" – he had not realized it before.

Women and children and young and old men flee from the shooting. You can see the police on top of the armoured cars. The one on the right is holding a revolver.

When the shooting started, the crowd turned to run; the shooting continued into their backs. One young woman fell and her companion went back to help her. As he turned her over he saw that her chest had been shot away. She was dead. A little boy ran, holding an old black coat over his head as if it

would protect him from the bullets. The shooting seemed to go on and on; police standing on the top of a Saracen car shot in wide arcs from the hip, stopping only to reload their revolvers or Sten guns. The people ran and ran and fell. Eventually the shooting stopped. It had lasted forty seconds or more. 705 rounds were fired.

The square and the roads and the field around the police station were empty of moving things. There was no crowd now; only scattered bodies, in grotesque positions, lying as they had fallen. Sitting at home, one young Sharpeville mother, who had sent her husband to listen to the announcement, knew that something terrible had happened. As she ran towards the square outside the compound, she thought she could see fallen sheep lying on the ground. As she came nearer, she realized they were people. Among them were children and old men, women and passers-by. One of those killed had been delivering invoices for his firm, some distance from the police station, when his head was blown off.

The wounded wait for attention, while the police stand around in small groups. Notice the pile of hats that have been gathered up. What do they suggest to you?

As Joshua Motha lay on the ground, unable to move, the police surveyed the scene. White and African police emerged from the gates of the compound but offered no help to the injured and dying. The Rev. Robert Maja, a Presbyterian Minister in Sharpeville, also came on the scene. As he went from body to body, people recognized him; they asked him for water, and complained of the heat from the sun. He brought

them water, having borrowed a big empty bottle from a neighbour, and he tried to make rough covers from their clothes, to keep off the worst of the heat. Among the dead were members of his congregation, including Sepampoerre, an old man.

Meanwhile, a white policeman had ordered Joshua Motha to get himself out of the way as there was nothing wrong with him and, if he did not move, he might end up being killed. As Motha tried to rise, he realized that his leg was hanging loose and something was sticking out. But now the trucks were coming to remove the bodies and a policeman suggested that they phone for some ambulances as well. Motha was pulled out of the way by some police, then helped by a friend across the square to the clinic fence, where he waited for the ambulance.

Humphrey Tyler began to search among the dead and dying for evidence of weapons. He found some shoes, some hats and a few bicycles among the bodies. A little later the ambulances and the trucks arrived. Eleven ambulances took the wounded away to be treated. Two truck-loads of bodies were taken to the mortuary. By about half past two the dead, dying and injured had been removed. At 4 o'clock the rain came and washed the blood away from the stones outside the police station.

Humphrey Tyler went home to write his account of what had happened. It never appeared in the South African newspapers, but it was published in England the following Sunday.

South Africa that week

As the inhabitants of Sharpeville began to come to terms with the massacre, the people at Langa, in the Western Cape, prepared to attend a meeting at which the P.A.C. protest against the pass laws was to be discussed and at which they fully expected the authorities to agree to abolish the laws. About 10,000 came to the meeting, unaware that all public gatherings had been banned. The police ordered them to disperse, but few heard the three-minute warning. The police charged the crowd and were met with a hail of stones. The order was given to fire and two Africans were killed and forty-nine injured. The people reacted angrily and that night burned symbols of government authority, such as public buildings, in the township.

Over the next few days the government issued a series of statements giving their account of the shootings at Sharpeville. On 22nd March, the South African Prime Minister, Dr Verwoerd, explained that the riots of the day before had had nothing to do with passes and nothing to do with poverty or low wages. According to him, they were just a periodic phenomenon, which might occur anywhere in the world. In thanking the police for the courageous way in which they had handled the situation, he denied that they had used excessive force and thought they had behaved in an exemplary manner.

Taking up this theme of the reliability of the police, the Department of External Affairs assured the world on 26th March that a planned demonstration of about 20,000 natives had attacked the police with an assortment of weapons, including firearms. The demonstrators had shot first and it was only in self-defence that the police had fired, in an attempt to avert an even worse tragedy. Government supporters, too, emphasized the self-control of the police. When the Bishop of Johannesburg asked why the police had not fired only to wound and not to kill, the *Johannesburg Star* replied that, since 80 per cent of the wounded had been hit below the waist, the police had obviously not been firing to kill. Every shot could have killed a native if the police had wished to do so, argued the *Star*.

The Bishop of Johannesburg and other white liberals became concerned at the different statements which were being issued by the authorities and which suggested increasingly that the crowd at the police station had been armed and

Trucks carry the coffins of the dead to be buried together in the cemetery of Sharpeville. The people of Sharpeville line the route as their brothers and sisters are carried past.

The point of the protest is not lost even at the funerals. Two women carry a poster demanding Africa for Africans and an end to the passes.

violent. These statements were being reproduced uncritically not only in South African newspapers but also abroad. On the Wednesday morning, with promises from white liberals organized by the Bishop to pay for legal aid, lawyers began taking statements from the injured who were still in hospital. A number of the wounded had already been removed to cells by the police and charged with public order offences. The lawyers also arranged for an independent doctor to attend the post-mortem examinations on the dead. It was his evidence which succeeded in establishing the numbers of dead who had been shot in the back.

The authorities' claim that the crowd had been armed was soon dropped in the face of overwhelming evidence to the contrary.

Increasingly, among white South Africans, the debate became one not of whether the police had had the right to fire on an unarmed crowd but of whether the behaviour of the crowd had justified their firing. Most agreed with Lt. Col. Pienaar's view that "the native mentality does not allow them to gather for a peaceful demonstration. For them to gather means violence." Only a few were of the opinion – which was later expressed by the Bishop of Johannesburg and his counsel at the Commission of Enquiry – that there had been no justification for the conduct of the police. The majority of white South Africans were quite confident that there had been.

Black leaders, of course, took a different view. On 22nd March, the P.A.C. issued a statement in which they reaffirmed their commitment to non-violent protest and suggested that the shooting of unarmed civilians by the police confirmed the P.A.C. belief that South Africa was a police state which ruthlessly denied basic human rights to the vast majority of its indigenous people. The shooting also had the effect of uniting all the African organizations in horror and protest. Chief Albert Luthuli, the leader of the African National Congress (A.N.C.), publicly burnt his pass on 26th March and urged all other Africans to follow his example. Thousands of Africans stopped work in Cape Town, and 28th March was designated a day of mourning when all Africans were urged to stay at home. The pass laws were suspended and it seemed for a short time as though the long and bloody campaign had achieved something after all.

Then, on 30th March, the government declared a State of Emergency. Arrests began. Leader after leader of the opposition groups was taken to jail, white as well as black. Robert Sobukwe and Chief Luthuli were among the best known, but people who had not been active in politics for fifteen years were also woken in the early hours of the morning and placed in detention.

Hearing of the mass arrests, the Africans at Langa decided to take action. Led by a young student, Philip Kgosana, who was a member of the P.A.C., they marched to Cape Town and the Parliament Building. There were about 30,000 of them. The Chief of Police was at a loss as to how to cope with this huge, utterly peaceful crowd. The world's press were gathered

Albert Luthuli in the early 1960s. He was a prominent member of the African National Congress who had been detained and banned many times for his activities. In 1960, shortly after the Sharpeville emergency, he publicly burned his pass, for which he was detained again. In 1961 he received the Nobel Peace Prize for his anti-Apartheid activities. He died after being hit by a train in 1967, at the age of 69.

in Cape Town – a contrast to the situation at Sharpeville – and any repetition of police violence would increase the problems South Africa was already facing internationally.

To the twenty-three-year-old Kgosana, it was most important not to create a situation where the thousands of Africans following his leadership would be slaughtered. To him, as to Robert Sobukwe, non-violence meant not provoking violence as well as not offering it. When the Chief of Police promised him an interview with the Justice Minister, if he ordered the demonstrators to return home, Philip Kgosana accepted. By 4 o'clock the crowd was marching back to Langa. At 4.45 that afternoon Philip Kgosana was arrested as he returned for his appointment with the minister.

Philip Kgosana is held aloft by his supporters during their march on Cape Town on 30th March, 1960.

The State of Emergency regulations prevented news of his arrest being published. As far as his followers were concerned, he had simply disappeared. Within two days the African townships of Langa and Nyanga had been surrounded by police and army. Electricity and water were cut off. Troops stood by, armed with rifles and machine guns, as the police went in to break the strike. Africans were whipped on to the buses that took them to their work, or were taken off under arrest. Even so, it took four days of immense brutality to break the strike around Cape Town.

Elsewhere, the first days of April were filled with spreading strikes and public burnings of passes, but the government was now firmly in control. The death toll continued to rise. By 9th April, 83 non-white civilians and three non-white policemen had died; 365 non-white civilians and 26 non-white policemen had been injured. There were no white casualties. The black townships were patrolled ceaselessly by armoured Saracen cars carrying armed police. Only a few days earlier, one of the women injured at Sharpeville had explained that she had been present at the demonstration because she had wanted to see a Saracen; now it was highly unlikely that any African, man, woman, or child, would not know what one looked like.

Government repression culminated in the banning of the Africans' political organizations, the A.N.C. and the P.A.C., which were said to constitute a serious threat to the safety of the public.

The African movements had not proved strong enough on their own to change the system, but, perhaps, with international help, they might manage to.

Meanwhile, in Sharpeville, Constance and Ethel Maisilo were busy trying to face a future without their husbands, who were brothers both killed at the protest. The £80 a month that fed, clothed and housed their children would no longer be available. John Khots was a painter, but his right arm would not work any more. The machine gun bullets had shattered it. For 216 families and over 500 children, those forty seconds of gunfire were to mean a lifetime of almost unbearable difficulty.

Around the world

On Tuesday, 22nd March, the morning newspapers in Britain carried large headlines and as many details about the incident as they had been able to obtain. The headlines themselves indicated the difficulty of obtaining accurate information quickly and the way political views colour the selection of detail and fact. "56 Killed In Riot near Johannesburg" and "Mob Stones Armoured Car Force" ran the headlines in the Conservative *Times*. "Police Shoot Women in African Riots – The Massacre" read the labour *Daily Herald*.

South Africa was a member of the Commonwealth and its head of state was the Queen. Britain's economic links with the country went back to the early nineteenth century. The gold and diamonds for which South Africa was famous and the industries and banks of the South African economy were profitable investments. The constitution under which South Africa was governed had been drawn up at Westminster. All this meant that the shootings at Sharpeville were bound to receive prominent treatment in Britain.

When it became clear, following more independent accounts, that the shootings had been an unprovoked attack on a peaceful crowd, then reaction was swift. Richard Dimbleby, a leading television commentator, compared Sharpeville with Guernica, an undefended Spanish town destroyed by Nazi bombs in 1937. Other commentators were equally outraged, though more moderate in their comparisons. The *Daily Herald* called for a boycott of South African goods, which the A.N.C. had been demanding for some time, and it warned that the Africans' commitment to non-violent protest was being tested to the utmost by police action such as this. *The Times* was less certain and more bewildered, reflecting the Conservative viewpoint: while reacting against the violence, it could not condemn white governments or support radical movements with an easy conscience.

By lunchtime, over 600 people had gathered spontaneously outside South Africa House in Trafalgar Square, carrying placards condemning the shootings at Sharpeville. In the evening, a silent march was held through the streets of London.

In the House of Commons the differences in ideas and emphasis between Conservative and Labour members caused some sharp exchanges. The Conservative government refused

This is how the Daily Mirror *reported the shootings to its readers on the morning of 22nd March. Can you tell what its leader (editorial comment) would be from the headlines it has chosen?*

to be drawn on whether it would offer any financial help to victims (as it had done to victims of a mining disaster in the Orange Free State not long before) and strongly maintained that it would not interfere in South Africa's internal affairs. The Labour members sought a commitment to end the sale of military goods to South Africa, but on this, too, the government refused to be moved. Within a few days, however, as the scale of the tragedy became clear, the House did pass a resolution which expressed sympathy with South Africa at the tragic events. Although it sounded, and indeed was, a bland resolution, it marked a significant break from previous policy, where the government had firmly refused to make any comment at all.

Other countries were in a less ambiguous relationship with South Africa. The United States had only limited trading links and little past political involvement with the country in 1960 and so, as its own interests were not at stake, could issue an unequivocal statement condemning violence and recognizing as legitimate the grievances of the African people. While America was prepared to break its tradition of keeping silent on the internal affairs of other countries, only part of the impetus for doing so lay in the country's horror at the events at Sharpeville. The American statement was also partly a carefully considered response to the domestic difficulties being presented by black Americans campaigning for civil rights in the southern states of the U.S.A.

Another group of people, more concerned with self-interest than with high moral issues, reacted sharply to the news from Sharpeville. As black protest spread through the country and the South African government's ability to control the situation was called into question, international firms that had invested money in the South African economy withdrew their funds. Within three days, £90 million was wiped off share values on the Johannesburg stock exchange and, on 31st March, £70 million on a single day.

Protests poured in from governments and individuals all over the world. On 28th March, designated as a day of mourning by Chief Albert Luthuli, head of the A.N.C., flags flew at half mast in the Norwegian capital of Oslo. A banner reading "Embassy of Crime" was hung outside the South African Embassy in Brussels. In Wellington, New Zealand, there were demonstrations. Outside South Africa House in London more protest meetings were held, as they had been every day since Tuesday.

In India, the Lower House of Congress passed a resolution which expressed the deepest sympathy with those who had suffered and continued to suffer from discrimination and the policy of suppression of African people in their homeland. The government of Pakistan expressed its indignation at the indiscriminate killing.

For African countries, the events at Sharpeville were the final evidence, if any were needed, that the whites in South Africa were beyond the appeal of reason. Horrified by the pictures which were available throughout the world, black African states began to explore the possibilities of helping their fellow blacks in South Africa. They decided that they should appeal to the United Nations for a concerted international effort to bring the South African government to its

Women, men, children, black and white, old and young, demonstrate outside South Africa House in London the Sunday after the shootings, when a huge demonstration was organized in Trafalgar Square.

senses; to support their fellow Africans; and, hopefully, to arrive at some solution to the problems created by the white government, before the country sank into bloodshed.

The Security Council of the United Nations responded to their call and, on 1st April, 1960, with the exception of Britain and France, voted a strongly-worded resolution in which it recognized that the system under which blacks in South Africa were living was a "legitimate area of international concern" and a threat to world peace.

Still no word of regret, apology or sympathy with those hurt or bereaved came from the South African government. It continued to defend the actions of the police and offered no compensation to the survivors. The Bishop of Johannesburg pursued his demand for a Commission of Enquiry and when one was eventually set up, the words of his counsel summed up the view of the rest of the world:

> **The officers made no attempt to persuade the crowd by non-violent means to disperse.**
> **The officers failed to *order* the crowd to disperse.**
> **The officers failed to warn the crowd that if they did not disperse force would be used.**
> **The officers made no attempt to use any form of force less drastic than firearms.**
> **The officers failed to supervise and control the men under their command.**
> **The officers took no steps to ensure that if shooting started it would be limited and controlled and could be stopped.**
> **The constables started shooting without receiving an order to do so.**
> **Many of the constables shot to kill, not merely to wound.**
> **They did kill sixty-nine people including eight women and ten children.**
> **The shooting was indiscriminate and continued long after the crowd had turned and fled.**
> **The 180 wounded included thirty-one women and nineteen children.**
> **There was no justification for the police to open fire on the crowd and therefore no justification for the conduct of the police.**

This was the verdict that many ordinary people all over the world accepted. Their view of South Africa and of its ideology was irrevocably altered. Their humanitarian concern ensured perhaps more than any action of governments or international organizations that the name Sharpeville and the events of that March day would not be forgotten.

THE INVESTIGATION

Why was the protest organized?

The pass laws and Apartheid In 1948, white South Africans elected a Nationalist government which was committed to a policy of Apartheid, or separate development. At its most fundamental, this was a policy which saw black South Africans as a constant and cheap source of labour for the white population, whose economic well-being would be assured as a result. The pass laws were to be extended and developed as a major tool in enforcing this policy.

Every black who lives outside the areas reserved for African habitation (the *bantustans*) and who is over the age of 16 must carry a pass book. This pass book contains sections for the following information and documents:

1. Residential address; labour bureau where registered; official permit to remain in, or go to, a specific area; and any referrals to Aid Centres (i.e. offences against the pass laws)
2. Employer's name and address and signature for each week
3. Tax receipts
4. Concessions, exemptions and privileges
5. Driver's licence
6. Weapons licence
7. Identity document with sex, name, ethnic classification, photograph and Reference Book (pass) number, and fingerprints.

Enforcing the pass laws People must produce their pass books on demand. Anyone who cannot, or whose pass book is not in order, can be heavily fined, imprisoned, forced to enter low-paid work, or "endorsed out" – that is, he or she may have the right to live and work in an area taken away and be forcibly returned to the *bantustans*.

Between 1948 and 1981 approximately 12.5 million people, according to the government, were arrested or prosecuted under the pass laws. This is probably an under-estimate. The second half of the 1950s was a particularly active time for such prosecutions; over a million and a quarter people were endorsed out of the "white" urban areas and returned to the over-crowded and poverty-stricken parcels of land allocated to African people under the Native Land Act of 1913.

Passes in the past

This was a pass issued in 1903 in the Transvaal. It was this system of passes that was put into force throughout South Africa, and for every black South African, after the Nationalist victory in the 1948 election.

As long ago as 1809, the British colonial government at the Cape (the first British colony in Africa, extending around modern-day Cape Town) had introduced a law which required the Khoi-Khoi people to carry passes. The Khoi-Khoi were the original inhabitants of this area, but only those who were working for a white master were entitled to these passes. Any Khoi-Khoi without a pass could be arrested as a vagrant and made to serve on a white farm. Any white man could demand to see a pass at any time and arrest anyone failing to produce one.

The system was introduced in response to a rise in the price of slaves. White farmers could no longer afford to buy slaves

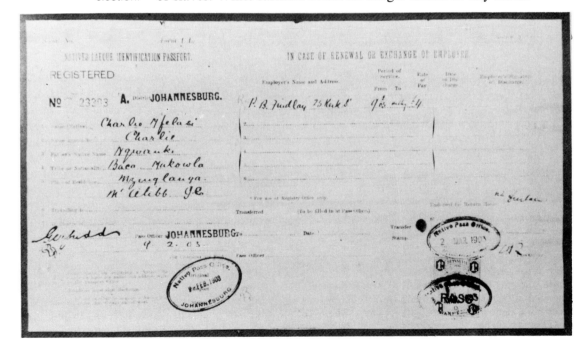

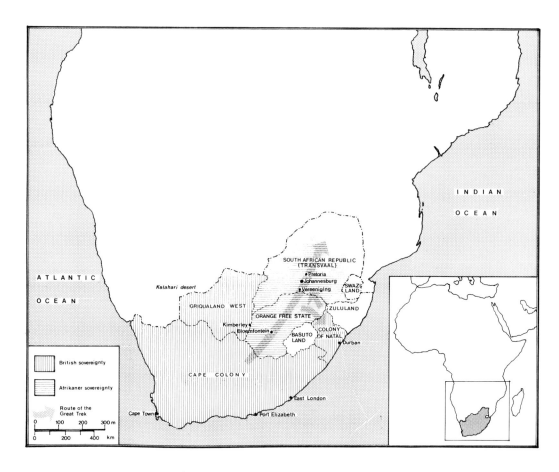

South Africa in the 1850s.

and wanted to have access to cheap, permanent labour. The law on passes effectively forced the Khoi-Khoi to work for white masters and created a system of "pass-slavery", as there were no regulations covering their wages (many were paid nothing at all) and if they moved from their employer they lost their pass.

This law was repealed in 1828, when Khoi-Khoi and other free people of the Cape were given limited political and economic rights. But it had set a pattern for labour control on the South African peninsula which has continued to the present day.

The Great Trek   The British had come into possession of this area of southern Africa during the wars against Napoleon. They were not the first whites to be interested in the Cape. In the seventeenth century, the Dutch East India Company had established a

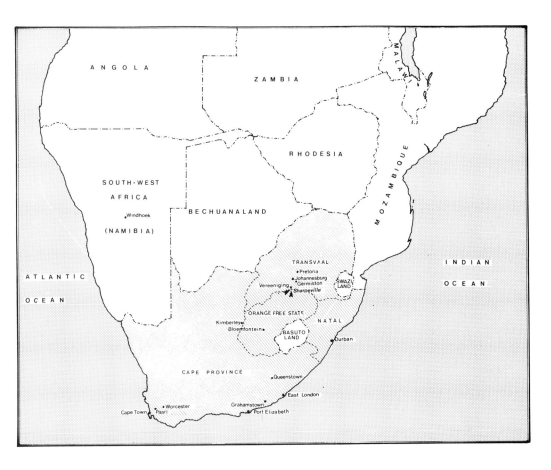

South Africa in the 1960s.

post here to victual its ships on the way to the East Indies, and from this start a small Dutch settlement had grown.

British policy from 1820, including the freeing of the slaves in 1834, was thought too liberal by the original Dutch settlers of the area. They organized an exodus from the Cape into the interior of southern Africa. It became known as the Great Trek.

Convinced of their own racial superiority, and certain that God had elected them to rule over the indigenous peoples of the region, the Dutch set out to establish their own country, free from British interference. Eventually they settled in the interior and by the 1850s had established two new states – the Orange Free State and the Transvaal. They called themselves Afrikaners – people of Africa.

The constitution of the Transvaal declared that there could be no equality between black and white. Pass laws based on the ones that had been in operation in the Cape were introduced, and "natives" were not permitted to walk on the pavements in Pretoria.

The first protests In 1906 the pass laws were extended to the Indian community, who had originally been brought to southern Africa in the 1860s by the British, to work on the Natal farms. This occasioned the first major protest against the laws. Led by Mohandas Gandhi (who was to become famous later as the leader of the Indian independence movement), the Indian and Chinese communities of Johannesburg pledged that they would refuse to register under the new act and would passively resist all attempts to force them to comply with it. By July 1907 only 500 out of 13,000 Transvaal Indians had registered. The authorities responded by arresting and imprisoning many Indians, but the protests continued and in 1908 the first

Gandhi in about 1903; photographed outside his office when he was practising law in South Africa, and beginning to organize the struggle of the Indian people against the white authorities of the Transvaal.

symbolic pass-burning took place at a huge meeting in Johannesburg.

The Transvaal government continued to implement legislation against the Indians, including a poll tax and a law which declared only Christian marriages to be legal. This brought Indian women into the struggle. When a group of Indian women were badly treated by the authorities after their arrest at a peaceful protest, Indian workers began a series of strikes. In 1913 the government was forced to give way; it abolished the poll tax, restored the legal status of Indian married women and repealed the pass laws against the Indians.

Women lead the struggle

In 1913, the Orange Free State passed a law which empowered local town councils to force South African black women to carry passes. Hitherto, only the men had had to do so. The women of the towns affected by the new law mounted a massive campaign of passive resistance. They refused to carry passes, and hundreds were sent to prison. In some places the jails became so full that the authorities could not deal with the protest. The struggle went on for nearly ten years. In 1920 the newspaper of the African National Congress reported that over a hundred women had been sent to jail for refusing to pay the fines imposed for not carrying passes. Eventually their struggle was successful: in 1922 the Orange Free State repealed the law.

Perhaps inspired by the example of the women, in 1919 male South African blacks in the Transvaal mounted their first campaign of passive resistance to the pass laws. From then on, organized protest against the pass laws was a recurring feature of black opposition to the South African government.

The pass laws in the 1950s

Early in the 1950s, the Nationalist government of South Africa passed a series of acts which made explicit the ideas of the Afrikaner community as to the place and function of blacks throughout the country. The Bantu (as all people of African descent were called by the Nationalist government) were regarded as having no permanent place in urban or in much of rural South Africa. The Native Land Act of 1913 had set aside small areas in which Africans were allowed to live and own land. These areas were now designated by the South African government as *bantustans*, or African homelands, and Africans could only live and work outside them if their work was economically necessary for the organization and servicing of white communities. As soon as they became economically

The first mass demonstration against the pass laws by black African men took place in 1919, following the successful attempts of their wives and sisters to resist the pass.

"useless" – i.e. unemployed or old or sick – their permission to live outside the native areas could be withdrawn. Massive forced removals of black families to the *bantustans* took place. Whole living areas, such as Sophia Town near Johannesburg, were pulled down and the residents forced out. Families were divided, as men might be awarded passes permitting residence in the black urban areas, but women and children were not.

Women on the march again

In 1956 the Nationalist government extended the pass laws to women. On 9th August, 20,000 women marched on the government offices in Pretoria to protest. Led by Lily Nguni, a member of the African National Congress, Helen Joseph, a white social worker and member of the Congress of Democrats, and Rahima Moosa of the South African Indian Congress, they delivered a huge petition to the Prime Minister's Office (the Prime Minister refused to meet them) and then held a silent protest outside the government complex.

The African National Congress

The A.N.C. was founded in 1912 by a group of educated, intellectual Africans, supported by clergymen and the chiefs of the people. Despite setbacks and difficulties, the organization

Campaigning against the pass and the pass laws was a central feature of black resistance from 1919 on. Here the people of Soweto organize a pass burning as part of a national campaign in 1956.

The bantustans, or "homelands", consist of many small and scattered pieces, based on the Native Land Acts. Today the land allocated to the blacks is about 13.6% of the total. Black Africans make up about 70% of the population.

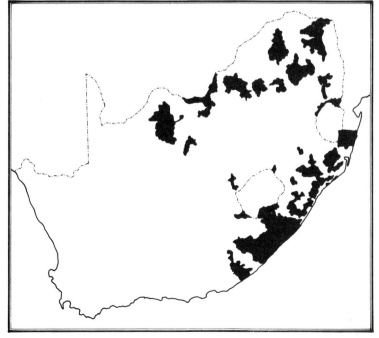

9th August, 1956: Lily Nguni, Helen Joseph and Rahima Moosa lead the protest of about 20,000 women to the Union Building in Pretoria to protest against the introduction of passes for women. (see page 34.)

remained the most unified and determined opponent of the supremacist policies of successive white governments. After the Second World War the A.N.C. emerged, under a new, young leadership, as the most vocal and determined opponent to Apartheid.

It was the A.N.C. that organized and led the Defiance Campaign of the early 1950s against the new laws of the Apartheid regime. It was the A.N.C. that forged the alliance with Indians, trade unions, coloured people (the category used by the government to classify people of mixed race, and descendants of the Khoi-Khoi, San and Malay slaves) and radical whites to launch the Freedom Charter, describing the fair and multi-racial society that was the goal of the Congress Alliance. As a result of its success, its leaders were banned, imprisoned and put on trial for treason.

The Africanist movement

As the laws against Africans became more stringent, and the government's attack on its leaders weakened the A.N.C., Africans began to feel a sense of impatience and anger with the A.N.C.'s methods, for these had produced not a single modification in the policies of the Nationalist government. A group of young men within the A.N.C. began campaigning for a change of policy and direction. They were "Africanists", who rejected the traditional A.N.C. position of forging alliances with all those opposed to Apartheid, whatever the colour of their skin. They were suspicious of the South African Communist Party which, although technically banned, continued to work with the A.N.C. in the struggle to defeat Apartheid.

"Africanism" had a very direct appeal to some sections of the black population. It demanded South Africa for the Africans, a policy in stark and simple contrast to the white South Africa policies of the Nationalist government. It also enabled black South Africans to identify themselves with the members of independence movements in other parts of colonial Africa, struggling for (and achieving) self-government.

In November 1958 the Africanists left the A.N.C. and set up their own organization called the Pan-African Congress. Led by the forceful and able Robert Sobukwe, it adopted a programme which aimed to establish a government "of the African, by the African, for the African" and which rejected the "multi-racial liberalism" of the A.N.C.

The pass law protests of March 1960

In December 1959 both the A.N.C. and the P.A.C. held their annual conferences. Both decided to mount a campaign against the pass laws. The A.N.C. set anti-pass day as 31st March, 1960; the P.A.C. announced that its supporters should invite arrest, accept jail sentences and, if released, seek re-arrest. The protests were to be non-violent. Their slogan was "No bail, no defence, no fine". They hoped as a result to disrupt totally the system through which the pass laws were administered.

On 18th March the P.A.C. launched its campaign and called for nationwide demonstrations to be held on the 21st. In Sharpeville thousands were to respond to the call.

Why did the police shoot?

When the police opened fire on the crowd of Sharpeville residents gathered outside the police station, there was no sense among them or the crowd, or, subsequently, among the South African people, that this represented a departure from accepted police practice. It was different in degree, perhaps, from other incidents in which black people engaged in protests against white laws had been shot, but few questioned the legality of the police action. For many years the South African police had had the operational powers to use firearms when their commanding officers deemed it appropriate.

Official figures of the numbers killed when police fired on black crowds

1917:	Grahamstown: White panic over Location (black area) demonstration:	2
1917:	Ouamboland: "Show of force" to tribesmen	38
1920:	Rand: African mineworkers' strike	8
1920:	Port Elizabeth: Protest over arrest	21
1921:	Queenstown: Religious community refusing to move	163
1922:	Namibia: Refusal to pay punitive Dog Tax	100
1925:	Bloemfontein: Punitive action in Location	5
1929:	Durban: Trade union office attacked	5
1930:	Durban: Pass-burning campaign	4
1930:	Worcester: "Show of strength" after A.N.C. meeting	5
1933:	Germiston: Protest meeting over permit raids	1
1942:	Pretoria: Wage protest	6
1946:	Johannesburg: African mineworkers' strike	9
1949:	Rand: Pass and beer raids	6
1950:	Witzieshoek: Rural protests	16
1950:	Rand: May Day protest	18
1952:	Port Elizabeth: Crowd revolt after shooting	9
1952:	Johannesburg: Crowd revolt	3
1952:	East London: Crowd revolt	8
1952:	Kimberley: Crowd revolt	14
1959:	Paarl: Protest over banishment	1
1959:	Durban: Beer hall demonstration	3
1959:	Windhoek: Protest over Location removal	11
1960:	Sharpeville: Anti pass law protest	69

Racial supremacy   The Dutch colonists who first settled at the Cape in 1652 developed an attitude to the black inhabitants of the area which was to have a profound effect on the history of this part of the world.

On their arrival, the Dutch encountered two groups of people: the Khoi-Khoi and the San. The Khoi-Khoi were cattle-herders who also traded peacefully with their neighbours, such as the Xhosa, to the east. Their contact with the white settlers had disastrous consequences for them, since they

This drawing, by a Dutch artist in the seventeenth century, shows the Khoi-Khoi building their houses.

contracted smallpox from the newcomers; they had never been exposed to the disease and had built up no resistance to it. Thousands of them died, and many more were reduced to economic dependence on the settler community (see page 29). Their dependence encouraged the Dutch in their view of them as their inferiors; an attitude shared by all other white settlers.

The San people, who were hunters, were much more independent of the white settlers at first. But as the Dutch moved inland and began to mark out farms for themselves from the countryside surrounding the Cape, and to hunt the game upon which the San depended, the San's livelihood was threatened. In an attempt to protect their hunting grounds, the San attacked the settlers with their poisoned arrows. The Dutch defended themselves with superior weapons – firearms – and, as more and more of the San were killed, they were forced further and further in to the less hospitable areas bordering on the Kalahari desert. To the Dutch settlers, the San were enemies who attacked them unawares with silent weapons and who threatened their right to the land of which the Dutch were the registered owners. Other white groups on the Cape shared the view that the Dutch farmers were the absolute owners of the land and that the San had no rights to it.

The point which set apart the Dutch settlers' attitude to black people from that of other white groups on the Cape was their justification of it through their religious beliefs. English white settlers regarded black people as culturally, economically and intellectually inferior to themselves, but before the law the black man was entitled to equal treatment. It was not possible for English law to disadvantage a male petitioner because of the colour of his skin. The discrimination practised against black people was not institutional and could therefore often be overcome on a personal, if not on a national, basis.

To the Dutch settlers, however, white supremacy was not only desirable, it was sanctioned by the law of God. They believed in a form of Christianity based on the teachings of John Calvin, who held that God had pre-ordained which people should share eternal life with Him. These people are known as the "Elect". The Dutch settlers used the Bible to show to their satisfaction that people with non-white skins were not of the Elect. Thus, the black people of the Cape could not claim to be equal with the whites.

The Boer republics As the ties of the Dutch settlers with their parent country became looser, their attitudes and religion became more and more distinctive. They regarded themselves as belonging to Africa – "Afrikaners" – and they had their own language – Africaans – developed from the Dutch of their ancestors. When they established their own independent countries in the central area of southern Africa, they built into their legal systems and constitutions their religious and personal beliefs about the rights, responsibilities and superiority of white people (see page 31). As a result, the Transvaal and the Orange Free State were places where blacks lived and worked on suffrance and where they would never have any role in determining or contributing to the future.

On the other hand, white people were dependent on the services that black, and also Asian, people (originally brought to the country as little better than slaves), could perform. Inevitably, some members of these "inferior" groups were able to obtain an independent livelihood in the towns.

The mineral revolution When diamonds and later gold were discovered in southern Africa (1870 and 1886), the way of life that had been evolving over the previous hundred years changed very rapidly. In place of a predominantly rural society, where typically whites owned the land and blacks worked it, a complicated industrial urban society grew up that demanded more and more labour to survive and develop. By means of taxation and sometimes of kidnapping black workers were forced into the industrial areas, to do the hardest and most difficult jobs for very low wages. They were housed in "native compounds" resembling barracks or prisons.

The poorest of the white people also came to the industrial areas. Many were Afrikaners who could no longer eke out a living from the land. They came to the towns and lived among the black and Asian communities upon whom they depended for their livelihood. The old Afrikaner certainties were being threatened.

"No better than a kafir" That whites should control, dominate and manage blacks seemed self-evident to the Afrikaners. But they were now faced with a situation in which, in the words of a future leader of South Africa, poor white Afrikaners were living in conditions "no better than a kafir" – a term meaning a "heathen", used by Afrikaners to describe all black Africans. Some were worse off than "kafirs", as they were employed as servants in black households. Others were living with and marrying black South Africans and having children of mixed race. From an orthodox Afrikaner point of view, such a situation was

contrary to the will and the word of God. The more militant of them resolved to work for a South African society in which every Afrikaner could be assured of wealth and power greater than that of any non-Afrikaner. They formed a secret society called the "*Broderbond*", in order to achieve this goal.

The Union of South Africa In 1910, the two Afrikaner provinces and the British colonies of the Cape and Natal were united into a single country, the Union of South Africa. The constitution ensured that rural (primarily Africaans-speaking) areas of the country would have a built-in protection against the urban, English-speaking communities. It also ensured that no province could impose on any of the others its own ideas as to who should vote and who should not, for any change in the franchise had to have the agreement of a two-thirds majority in parliament.

In the long term, these conditions ensured that the Afrikaner whites would gain control of the government. In the long run the theories of the Afrikaners about the role and place of black and non-white South Africans in their country would be enshrined in the laws and principles of the Union.

Winning control For any party to win a general election in the Union and to remain in government, it was vital to have the support of the majority of the Afrikaner people. To win such support, all governments, to a greater or lesser extent, devised and implemented laws which would ensure the economic, legal and social superiority of the white communities. Thus, in 1924, the Afrikaner and Labour Parties worked together to win the election and were then able to reserve all skilled work in the mining industry for white workers and to bar black workers from jobs in the civil service and other "white collar" employment.

By 1936, the Afrikaner political parties were firmly in control. An act was passed which removed black voters from the electoral roll in the Cape province. (The two-thirds majority of the vote in parliament needed for this was easily gained.) Also, the land laws were strengthened, reducing the total area of land which black people had the right to own to only 13 per cent of the country. Black people made up over 70 per cent of the population.

Despite these successes, however, it seemed to many Afrikaners that their position was constantly being threatened by non-white communities. Throughout the years between the world wars, the main thrust of the legislation had been against black South Africans. The coloured communities of the Cape, the descendants of the Khoi-Khoi, the Malayan slaves and people of mixed race, were exempt from any of the discriminating laws and had equal political and economic rights with the Cape whites. The large Indian community in Natal, while disliked and mistrusted by the English communities there, was becoming increasingly prosperous.

During the almost worldwide depression of the 1930s the rural areas of South Africa were particularly hard hit. Rural white poverty appeared once more and large numbers of whites began to trek into the towns in the hope of earning a living there. Once again they found themselves at the bottom of the economic ladder, worse off than coloured and Indian families and no better off than many Africans. When, during the Second World War, black workers were admitted into skilled jobs because of labour shortages in key industries such as mining, the position of the poor urban whites was even more threatened. The only solution seemed to lie in some permanent and absolute application of the principles of difference or separateness: in a series of policies that would separate the people on earth as they were to be separated in heaven. The Afrikaner intellectuals responded with the policy of Apartheid: separate development. In 1948 the Nationalist Party, an Afrikaner party that supported the policy of Apartheid, was elected to govern South Africa.

Apartheid in practice   In 1950 a further election strengthened the position of the Nationalists. Throughout the 1950s the government passed act after act designed to define for ever the position of non-white people as subordinate to the whites. Everyone had to be entered on a racial register, which categorized people according to their "colour". To determine whether someone was white or non-white, tests were used such as seeing whether a comb would stand up in your hair. Where you could live, and with whom, were then decreed according to your colour. Many families were divided by these acts; mothers, children and fathers separated. The type of education to which you were entitled was determined by the colour of your skin. No non-whites could strike. No African could enter an urban area for more than 72 hours unless she or he had been born there and was permanently resident and in possession of a pass. Non-whites were excluded from white universities. It was a criminal offence to protest against these laws by breaking them, and severe penalties were imposed. The police could enter and search premises without a warrant, and the Criminal Procedure Act of 1955 extended police powers to kill a person

Apartheid in action. who was suspected of committing an offence, or was fleeing or resisting arrest. Black nurses were not allowed to treat white patients even in an emergency. Buses, park benches, cinemas and all public places were divided into those for whites only and those for non-whites. Anyone who opposed these laws was considered to be a Communist and could be "banned", that is, confined to a given area, forbidden to meet with people and forbidden from saying or writing anything about the state.

The shooting at The police at Sharpeville were faced with a crowd which was
Sharpeville undoubtedly breaking the law by engaging in a protest. The right of the police to shoot was reasonably established in law, provided that certain procedures were gone through and provided that their commanding officers were confident that the crowd could not be dispersed by other means. The targets at which they shot were not citizens of the state, with rights and legal protection. The order to shoot, if it was given, and the willingness of the police to carry it out were part and parcel of the ideology of Apartheid which the government of South Africa embraced.

Was the protest a failure?

For the A.N.C. and the P.A.C. On 8th April, 1960, the South African government introduced a bill into Parliament which declared the A.N.C. and the P.A.C. unlawful organizations and a serious threat to public safety. Under the Suppression of Communism Act, passed in 1950, the penalty for supporting or "furthering the aims" of these organizations was imprisonment for up to ten years. Only sixteen members of the all-white South African Parliament voted against the bill, 128 voting for it.

Mass arrests More arrests were made after 8th April, following those that had occurred when the State of Emergency had been declared (see page 19). No opponent of the government could feel safe. Some managed to escape to the High Commission Territories of Basutoland, Bechuanaland and Swaziland, or away to the north and Rhodesia, but many more were imprisoned. Over 100 whites and 2,000 non-whites were detained; some were subsequently released gradually, up to August 1960 when the "emergency" was declared ended. Many of those directly involved with the banned organizations or with the pass protests were tried and imprisoned. Robert Sobukwe was sentenced to three years; Albert Luthuli was fined £100 for burning his pass.

The A.N.C. goes underground Instead of disbanding, the P.A.C. and the A.N.C. announced their intention of carrying on as underground organizations. Plans for the new organizations had been laid while the leaders were in prison together during the emergency. The A.N.C. was to be led by a young Johannesburg lawyer called Nelson Mandela, who was currently one of the defendants in the "Treason Trial" which had been going on for four years since the Congress Alliance of 1956 (see page 36). On his release in March 1961, Mandela immediately began to tour the country, organizing protests and building up support for a strike to voice the demand for a National Convention of elected representatives of all races, men and women, whose job it would be to determine a new, non-racial and democratic constitution for South Africa. Warrants were issued for his arrest, but he successfully evaded the police with the help of his friends and supporters of the A.N.C., black and white alike.

Nelson Mandela. This photograph was taken in 1962, when he was in hiding and organizing Umkhonto and the A.N.C. He was known as the Black Pimpernel.

The call for a republic South Africa was a Crown Dominion, with the English monarch as Head of State. However, the Afrikaner, Nationalist government had long wanted to break the remaining constitutional ties with England by creating a republic in South Africa, with a President as Head of State. The idea of adopting republican status had been mooted by the Prime Minister of South Africa, Henrik Verwoerd, before the Sharpeville massacre, but the massacre and the international reaction to South Africa helped make the idea a more popular one, even among the English-speaking white communities.

Verwoerd had promised that if South Africa became a republic, he would still seek to keep it within the Commonwealth. But it was clear, after Sharpeville, that most Commonwealth countries would be hostile unless the Nationalists

Dr Henrik Verwoerd.

changed their racial policies. Ghana and India refused to consider the application for membership of South Africa as a republican country. Canada supported them. The Afrikaners were delighted. On 31st May, 1961, South Africa was declared a republic.

The Spear of the Nation The A.N.C.'s campaign for a National Convention was in response to the constitutional changes which would be involved in becoming a republic. The demonstrations, of which the government had been informed, were to take the form of a three-day stay-at-home strike, beginning on 29th

At the Commonwealth Conference in London the following year, leading figures in British and South African politics took part in a 72-hour vigil to remind the Commonwealth Prime Ministers of the deaths of 72 people in Sharpeville and Langa the year before. South Africa's application to remain in the Commonwealth was rejected at this meeting.

May and finishing on the day that South Africa was to become a republic. Informed beforehand by the protesters, the government tried to nip the strike in the bud. Towards the end of May, the police made large-scale arrests; thousands of Africans were imprisoned under the pass laws and meetings were banned throughout the country.

These police tactics had some success in making the strike less widespread than had been hoped. Its failure, combined with the government's response to Sharpeville and the white communities' willingness to use violence and intimidation against non-whites, was encouraging a fundamental reassessment of policy within the A.N.C. and the P.A.C. Abandoning their policy of non-violence, each organization formed a military wing, whose function was to commit acts of sabotage and whose purpose was to accelerate the collapse of the white state by violent means. *Poqo*, the military wing of the P.A.C., was prepared to use violence to endanger lives. *Umkhonto We Sizwe*, the military wing of the A.N.C., was committed to a policy of attacking selected installations only. Its leader and

Young supporters of Umkhonto We Sizwe receive their military training in the bush.

commanding officer, the person charged with training, establishing the organization, and determining the targets, was Nelson Mandela. On 16th December, 1961, *Umkhonto* blew up pylons and municipal offices in Johannesburg and Port Elizabeth.

Detention without trial

The government's response to the new militancy of the black communities was to introduce a series of increasingly severe laws, which enabled the police to arrest and detain anyone they suspected of being connected with a banned organization or an anti-government group. The police were not required to say who had been detained or what charges they faced. In May 1961, twelve-day detention without trial was introduced. In 1963, following the success of the A.N.C.'s campaigns, this period was extended to 90 days, and two years later to 180 days. The 90-Day Act also empowered the Minister of Justice to continue to detain certain categories of prisoners, who had been convicted of political offences, after the end of their sentences. The Minister used this to keep Robert Sobukwe in jail after he had completed his three-year sentence. He

49

remained in jail until 1969 and then was released under a banning order to Kimberley. He died there in 1979, still a "banned" person. Banned people cannot go to meetings, or meet with more than one person at once. They cannot go to school or college, cannot write articles for magazines, cannot be quoted and cannot leave the place to which the banning order confines them. The Minister of Justice can ban anyone, without applying to a court.

The draconian laws were regarded by the white community as the only means by which they could obtain information about the activities of people opposed to the government. The secrecy about who had been detained and the fact that the detainees were forbidden access to anyone outside made it possible for the police to use violent interrogation techniques and these were effective in producing testimony against others active against the regime. Torture, sometimes leading to death, of detainees while in police custody has been a regular occurrence since the 90-Day law was introduced.

The Rivonia Trial   In October 1963 Nelson Mandela and several of his comrades, black, white and Indian, were accused together of sabotage and of furthering the cause of Communism. In a dramatic and often moving trial, the statements of the accused told the story of the persecution of the African people in their own home-land and described the struggle for human rights in which they were all engaged. Found guilty of the charges against them, they were imprisoned for life.

South Africa   As the policy of the Nationalist government towards the black
isolated   population became understood outside the country, there was a growing international movement to bring pressure to bear upon South Africa to reverse that policy. Led by the newly independent countries of the post-war world, especially India and Ghana, the General Assembly of the United Nations raised the issue of Apartheid. The massacre at Sharpeville gave impetus to the movement and the U.N. Security Council called on South Africa to initiate measures to bring about racial harmony based on equality. The following year the General Assembly recognized Apartheid as a threat to inter-national peace and in 1963 the Security Council (with France and Britain abstaining) voted for the introduction of a volun-tary arms embargo against South Africa by all member states. In 1974, South Africa was suspended from the General Assembly.

Economic action

The anti-Apartheid movement campaigns in Britain for the ending of Apartheid in South Africa. It has co-ordinated several successful boycotts, including the boycott of Barclay's Bank, which resulted in the bank's withdrawing from South Africa in 1986. How successful do you think posters such as these are in encouraging a personal boycott of South African goods?

International statements of disapproval and abhorrence undoubtedly gave moral encouragement to the opponents of Apartheid. Bringing international economic pressure to bear on South Africa had a more important effect. South Africa was peculiarly vulnerable, as its two major earners of foreign currency, gold and diamonds, were totally dependent for their value on the international market, and much of its manufacturing and financial sectors were owned by foreign national companies. South Africa also needs to import oil. In the aftermath of Sharpeville there was a massive withdrawal of international finance. The value of the *Rand* (the South African unit of currency) fell drastically on the foreign exchange markets and millions of pounds were wiped off the value of shares. This was the result of the reaction of those responsible for investing foreign capital in South Africa, who were alarmed at the level of unrest and at the international revulsion following Sharpeville. However, the government of South Africa quickly showed that it had the authority and power to quell such disorder. By the mid-1960s all the lost capital had returned, and much new capital was pouring in. By the end of the 1960s the South African economy was stronger than it had ever been.

Anti~Apartheid Movement
13 Mandela St London NW1 0DW
01-387 7966

LOOK before you BUY

BOYCOTT *the products of APARTHEID*

Sanctions As early as 1959, Chief Albert Luthuli, the A.N.C. leader, had called for an international boycott of all South African goods, a call renewed after the Sharpeville massacre. Some countries, such as India, already supported and implemented such a boycott, or economic sanctions, as they became known. Others, including the United Kingdom, whose economic stake in South Africa was high, rejected it. But all over the world individuals and organizations began operating a personal boycott of South African goods. Although the dramatic isolation of South Africa which appeared to be occurring in the immediate aftermath of Sharpeville did not materialize, a number of small steps combined over the next fourteen years increasingly to cut off South Africa from the rest of the world. The arms embargo, the oil embargo endorsed by the Arab states in 1973, the progressive cutting of sporting links, and the ending of diplomatic relations by many nations have all made South Africa's position in the international community a unique one.

White communities in South Africa In 1961 the Nationalist government won its fourth whites-only general election in succession, against their main English-

This is a house for a white family in the lovely Cape Town suburb of Seapoint. The black woman in the picture is the maid.

speaking opponents, the United Party. In this election many English-speaking South Africans supported the Nationalist, Apartheid government for the first time. With very few exceptions, the reaction of the white communities to Sharpeville was to draw closer behind the defensive wall of Apartheid. Many felt that only the Nationalist government had the will to protect them from an apparently violent African population and a hostile outside world. Many years before, the forefathers of the Afrikaners, on the Great Trek, had successfully protected themselves from hostile Africans and hostile environments by using their ox-wagons to form a circle or *laager* of defence. The idea that this conveyed, of a closed, tight, defended world, held a powerful attraction for the white communities. And by the end of the 1960s it seemed that their faith in nationalism, Apartheid and force had proved justified. The South African whites enjoyed the highest standard of living of any group of white people in the world.

The consequences of Sharpeville

One writer described Sharpeville as the turning-point at which no-one turned. Despite the massive shock waves that rolled around the world as a result of the massacre of Africans

The massacre at Sharpeville gave impetus to campaigns to break sporting links with South Africa. Here students protest outside the University Parks in Oxford, where a South African Test Cricket Team were playing Oxford University in May 1960. South African cricket teams no longer tour this country. South Africa is banned from the Olympics and the World Games.

53

outside the police station, South Africa seemed to have suffered no long-term damage. Its most powerful friends, Britain, France and the United States, continued to defend the country, both economically and at the United Nations, even if drawing the line at an open endorsement of South African policies. The attempts by the African political parties, the A.N.C. and the P.A.C., to turn to policies of direct confrontation and violence were met by the more effective violence of the government, backed by the power of law; and by the middle years of the decade all the best-known African leaders were either in prison or had been forced to flee and organize abroad. The detention laws had effectively silenced and controlled legitimate black opposition to the regime. The white communities, far from examining the moral position of Apartheid, or listening to the growing world condemnation from many sources, were being rewarded for their faith in the system by material comfort and economic security. Sharpeville had shocked the world, but seemed to have changed nothing. By the end of the decade, everyone seemed to be agreed that Apartheid was a success, and the future of South Africa assured. The pass book still controlled the lives of most of the people living there.

Did the protest succeed?

Soweto, 1976 In June 1976, school students in Soweto began organizing a protest at the government's plans to make Africaans the language of instruction for half the subjects taught in schools in the black townships of South Africa. Conditions in black schools were already appalling. There were not enough books, there were not enough teachers, and the buildings were in a poor state of repair. All this contrasted sharply with the white education system, on which significantly larger sums of money were spent and which was one of the best equipped and staffed systems in the world.

Students in Soweto in 1976 protesting at the government's attempts to impose Africaans as the medium for teaching in their schools. On 16th June, 1976, the students of Soweto went on strike, as part of their protest against the introduction of Africaans. Few of their teachers could speak this language at all, let alone speak it well enough to instruct anyone through it.

As was usual on the occasion of black protests in the township, the police arrived armed and ready to use force if

necessary to assert their control. As the students were marching towards their rally the police opened fire. No-one knows how many died that day. At least 25 and probably more than 100 children were killed. Like Sharpeville years before, Soweto was to become a symbol of the struggle against Apartheid. As the protests spread across South Africa hundreds more were killed and thousands wounded by the police.

More than just death and international revulsion forged the links between the two protests. Shortly after the Soweto uprising the government passed an act which prevented anyone from bringing actions against the state for unlawful detention; and which further laid down that no court action could be brought against the state or any of its officials, who were acting in good faith to prevent or terminate internal disorder. This was the second such act: the first had been passed in 1961, in the aftermath of Sharpeville.

Black Consciousness The Soweto protests had their roots in the growth of the Black Consciousness Movement of the late 1960s. This movement developed partly to fill the vacuum of legal opposition left by the banning of the A.N.C. and the P.A.C. and partly as an intellectual response to the need to reassert the rights and dignities of blacks, so systematically destroyed under Apartheid. Recognizing the potential threat of the Black Consciousness organizations, such as the South African Students' Organization, the government banned them and arrested one of their most prominent leaders, Steve Biko. Steve Biko died in detention on 12th September, 1977.

Renewing the armed struggle Many young people fled from the townships during the uprisings in 1976 and joined the military training camps of *Umkhonto We Sizwe*, in the neighbouring African states. The A.N.C. began to reassert its leadership both at home and abroad, and campaigns were mounted for the release of Nelson Mandela who became the symbol of the black struggle for the end of Apartheid. The number of acts of sabotage committed inside the country began to increase. Since 1976 railway lines and, increasingly, police stations and army camps have been attacked. In 1980 the great Sasol oil refinery was blown up by the A.N.C.

The U.D.F. is formed In 1983 a number of different anti-Apartheid groups came together, under the name of the United Democratic Front, to fight against the proposals for a new constitution being put forward by President Botha. This constitution would give a subordinate role in government to Indians and coloureds. Drawing on the traditions of the A.N.C., the Black Consciousness Movement and the Congress Movements, which had organized the protests of the 1950s, the U.D.F., in a short space of time, had mobilized black, Indian and coloured opinion so successfully that the new constitution received virtually no support from these communities.

Economic crisis From the mid-1970s South Africa's economic position was less secure. Oil prices rose sharply and the price of gold was unpredictable. The world economy went into recession, and the urban unrest of the mid-1970s and later made foreign investors more hesitant to commit their funds. The result has been a steady rise in black urban unemployment, from 12 per cent in 1971 to 21 per cent in 1981, and there have been further increases since. These economic conditions have led to mounting levels of unrest and protest in the black communities. In 1984 the black townships of the Vaal triangle staged a protest against rent increases for their slum properties, which had been proposed by the town councils appointed by President Botha. 7,000 troops were sent in to occupy Sebokeng town-

A meeting of the United Democratic Front (U.D.F.) in the Cape in 1985. The U.D.F. was formed in August 1983 as a multi-racial umbrella organization with over 300 affiliated groups including community-based civic groups, trade unions, church and women's groups, youth and student organizations, sporting clubs and professional bodies. The total membership was estimated at over one million. The policy of the U.D.F. was to resist the minority white government under the slogan "Apartheid divides, U.D.F. unites."

ship, one of the places involved in the protest. A neighbouring township also joined in. It was called Sharpeville.

The occupation of black South Africa From that date, the majority of the black towns of South Africa have been permanently occupied by the security forces, a combination of police and army. In June 1985 a State of Emergency was declared, at first covering only part and later extending to the whole country. As the popular uprisings continued, the government took powers to control the press, particularly reporting by foreign correspondents in South Africa. (It already had extensive powers over the domestic media.) As a result, it has become more difficult to establish with accuracy the extent of continuing protest, and the numbers of people killed and in detention.

In 1987 President Botha held a general election. His policies and approach to dealing with anti-Apartheid protests were supported by the electorate, while those white intellectuals who had begun to have doubts about the extent of force being used by the government were resoundingly defeated.

Outcomes Given the crisis South Africa has faced since 1985, it is easier for us to see now that Sharpeville was not quite the pointless tragedy we might have judged it to be in the late 1960s. As a result of the massacre, the black resistance movements began to explore new ways of fighting the regime. Though these have never seriously challenged white power, they have succeeded in maintaining a political credibility which has given those opposed to Apartheid an organizational focus to which to relate. The A.N.C. is still regarded by leaders in South Africa and abroad as the legitimate expression of black political aspirations, and even white South African businessmen have met with the A.N.C., recognizing it as the future government of South Africa. Had the A.N.C. not taken the path of illegality, after being banned in 1960, it is unlikely that it would be the force it is today in South African politics.

Following the Sharpeville massacre, the South African government decided to abandon its previous policy of containing black opposition through a conventional framework of law; instead it adopted a series of coercive measures which deprived black citizens and whites opposing the regime of many basic human rights. As a result of this, it became increasingly difficult for western governments to defend and support the South African government, at least openly, and after 1985 South Africa came under increasing international pressure. By the late 1980s only Britain, Japan and Germany refused to implement any significant policy of sanctions.

Where freedom flowers

Since Sharpeville, thousands of black people of all ages have been killed by the South African security forces as the white communities attempt to retain power. One of them was Hector Peterson, who was the first child to die in the Soweto protest in 1976. He was thirteen. Another was Ruth First, a white woman working in Mozambique and who had been committed to a democratic multi-racial South Africa since the 1950s. She was murdered in 1982 by South African guerrillas operating across the border. Another to die was Solomon Mahlangu, a member of *Umkhonto We Sizwe*, who was hanged in 1977 for his part in bringing the armed struggle into South Africa. The night before he died he sent a message to his mother: "My blood will nourish the tree which will bear the fruits of freedom. Tell my people that I love them and that they must continue the struggle. Do not worry about me, but about those who are suffering." Solomon Mahlangu was twenty-one.

South African troops and police occupy Tsakane township in June 1985. Troops are still in occupation of the townships.

President Botha.

Important dates in South African history

1000 on: Sotho and Nguni states well established in central plateau and on eastern seaboard
1486: Khoi-Khoi have first contact with Portuguese explorers
1497: Nguni have first contact with Portuguese explorers
1652: Dutch settlement at Cape
1779: First Xhosa War
1780: Great Fish river claimed by Dutch as eastern boundary of colony
1795: British occupy Cape
1806: Re-occupation of Cape by British
1828: Citizenship granted to "all free persons of colour" in Cape
1834: Emancipation of slaves at Cape
1836: Great Trek
1838: Battle of Blood River: Zulus defeated by Trekkers and African allies
1860: First Indian indentured labour brought to Natal

1867: Diamonds discovered
1880: First Boer War
1881: British defeated at Majuba Hill: Transvaal returned to Boers
1886: Gold discovered in the Rand
1894: Glen Grey Act
1899–1902: Second Boer War
1906: Indian Pass Law in Natal
1910: Union of four colonies

1912: A.N.C. founded
1913: Native Land Act
1919: A.N.C. pass-burning campaign
1920: African miners' strike
1922: White miners' strike: Rand revolt
1925: The Wage Act
1926: Colour Bar Act
1927: Hostility Act
First African trades union founded in Rand
1936: Native Representation and Land Acts
1938: Voortrekker Centenary celebrations
1943: First Alexandra bus strike
1946: Great African miners' strike: many killed and injured and leaders arrested
1948: Election of Nationalist government: Implementation of Apartheid

1950: Suppression of Communism Act: Registration Act aimed at classifying the population by colour and race

1952: Defiance Campaign
1953: Bantu Education Act
1955: Adoption of Freedom Charter
1956: Cape Coloured removed from voters' role
Treason Trial commences
1959: P.A.C. formed
1960: Sharpeville and Langa massacres:
A.N.C. and P.A.C. banned
State of Emergency

1961: South Africa becomes a republic, outside the Commonwealth
Last of Treason Trial defendants found not guilty
Umkhonto We Sizwe founded
1962: Sabotage Act: Sabotage becomes a capital offence; house arrest for banned persons
1963: 90-day detention
Rivonia Trial begins
1964: Rivonia defendants sentenced to life imprisonment
Transkei (Bantustan) given legislative assembly
1965: 180-day detention
1973: Wave of strikes by black workers
1974: Internal Security Act passed
1976: Death of Steve Biko in police detention
Soweto Massacre: widespread uprisings
1980: Launch of campaign to release Nelson Mandela
Oil-refinery near Durban damaged in major A.N.C. guerrilla attack
1981: 20th anniversary of Republic
1982: Security Laws strengthened: Defence Act allows massive increase of expenditure on police and armed forces
1983: U.D.F. formed
Constitutional changes proposed
1984: New constitution implemented
Widespread uprisings
1985: COSATU formed
1986: Nationwide State of Emergency
South African business leaders meet A.N.C. in Zambia
1988: U.D.F. and 17 opposition organizations (including the Detainees' Parents Support Commitee) banned

Further reading

THE EVENTS

Ambrose Reeves, *Shooting at Sharpeville*, Gollancz, 1960. (This is the fullest account of the shootings and contains verbatim evidence given by witnesses to the Commission of Enquiry.)

THE INVESTIGATION

J. Barber, *South African Foreign Policy 1945–70*, OUP, 1973
M. Benson, *South Africa: The Struggle for a Birthright* (History of the ANC), Penguin, 1966
D. Denoon, *South Africa since 1800*, Longman, 1972
R. First, J. Steele and C. Gurney, *The South African Connection: Western Investment in South Africa*, London, 1972
S. Harris, *Timeline: South Africa*, Dryad Press, 1988
D. Harrison, *The White Tribe of Africa*, BBC, 1981
E. Roux, *Time Longer Than Rope*, University of Wisconsin, 1964

Index